# THE ENCYCLOPEDIA
## OF
# BRAVE WARRIORS

## WARRIORS & WEAPONS IN FACTS & FIGURES

BY ARTEM ZIBALOV

ILLUSTRATED BY NATALIA BOLDYRIEVA

PUBLISHING HOUSE

RANOK

**The Encyclopedia of Brave Warriors**
**Warriors & Weapons in Facts & Figures**
Series: Infographics for Kids



Created in 2018 by Encyclopedias team.
First published in 2018 by Publishing House Ranok Limited.
Redesigned for global publishing by Luda Werdin in 2019.
Luda Werdin is the official representative of Publishing House Ranok Limited authorized to act on its behalf.

ISBN: 978-617-09-5787-0

Publishing House Ranok Limited
135-27 Kibalchicha street, Kharkiv, Ukraine, 61071
"Encyclopedias" is a division of Publishing House Ranok Limited
For more information, contact "Encyclopedias",
21a Kosmichna street, Entrance 1, Floor 6,
Kharkiv, Ukraine, 61145
Email: office@ranok.com.ua
Edited by Anastasiia Tolmachova
Book design by Natalia Boldyrieva

# CONTENTS


WARRIORS OF ANCIENT ASSYRIA ... 4

SCYTHIANS ... 6

ROMAN LEGIONARIES ... 8

VIKINGS ... 10

MEDIEVAL KNIGHTS ... 12

MONGOL ARMY ... 14

JAPANESE SAMURAI ... 16

15TH CENTURY SWISS ... 18

UKRAINIAN COSSACKS ... 20

SWEDISH INFANTRY ... 22

NAPOLEON'S GRENADIERS ... 24

FRENCH FOREIGN LEGION ... 26

US MARINES ... 28

BRITISH SPECIAL FORCES ... 30

# WARRIORS OF ANCIENT ASSYRIA

## Lance

A widely used weapon in the Assyrian army. It was made of a long pole and a metal head.

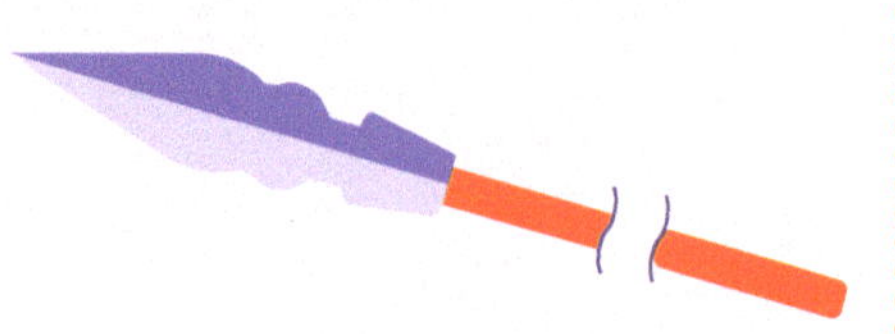

## Sling

A very simple device made from a piece of rope for throwing stones.

The ancient state of Assyria existed for about two millennia (24th — 7th centuries B.C.). In search of power, its kings organized and improved the army, and waged endless wars. To remain invincible, the army had to constantly perfect. At first, it consisted only of infantry and combat chariots but later it developed cavalry — the warriors who fought mounted on horses. The cavalry made the Assyrian army invincible.

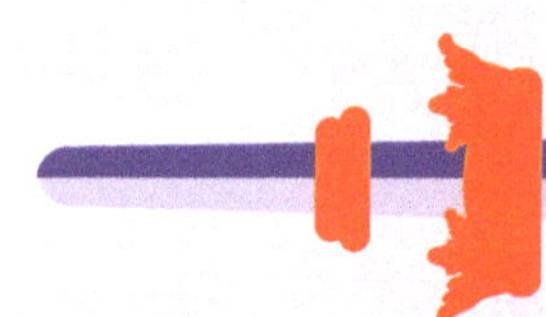

## Assyrian sword

Assyrians were one of the first to start making metal swords. The weapon turned out to be stronger, lighter, and sharper than that of bronze used by the enemies of Assyria.

## IMPORTANT DATES

**14th century B.C.**
The Assyrian army appears. The first aggressive campaigns.

**743–735 B.C.**
King Tiglath-Pileser III defeated the state of Urartu.

**727–722 B.C.**
King Shalmaneser V's reign. Israel campaigns.

**671 B.C.**
King Esarhaddon conquered Egypt.

**669–627 B.C.**
King Ashurbanipal's reign.

**612 B.C.**
The end of the Assyrian Empire.

# ASSYRIAN INFANTRYMAN

## ASSAULTING THE TOWN

# FAMOUS WARRIORS

### Tiglath-Pileser III

The king who changed the army. It was during his reign that cavalry was created, and ordinary armed peasantry turned into brave warriors.

### Sennacherib

The king whose whole reign was spent in wars. He suppressed the riots in subject territories and fought Israel and Palestine.

# SCYTHIANS

## Akinakes

Today, this Scythian sword might seem too short, as it was only about 2 feet long.

## Gorytos

A Scythian wooden case for the bow and arrows.

It was in ancient times that the steppes adjacent to the Black Sea coast were inhabited by various tribes. In the 7th century B.C., the nomadic people of Scythians came to live there. They were known for being invincible warriors, especially the cavalry. Perfectly protected with armor, their riders were well-trained and were not only good at archery but also at hand-to-hand combat. What's more, they cared about their horse's harness as much as about their own armor.

## Scythian armor

To protect the body from wounds, Scythians wore leather iron-sheathed shirts.

# IMPORTANT DATES

**7th century B.C.**

The Great Scythian Campaign to the Middle East that lasted for 26 years.

**514–513 B.C.**

Persian invasion to the Scythian lands.

**4th century B.C.**

Wars between Scythians and Macedonians

**3rd century B.C.**

Sarmatians forced Scythians out to the Crimea.

**2nd–1st centuries B.C.**

Wars between Scythians and Greeks in the Crimea.

**3rd century A.D.**

The Goths defeated the Scythian army.

# SCYTHIAN CAVALRY WARRIOR

## POTTERY FROM KUL-OBA KURGAN

# FAMOUS WARRIORS

### King Idanthyrsus

A brave and clever leader of Scythians. He is famous for defeating the enormously huge army of the Persian king Darius I by avoiding open combat for a long time.

### King Ateas

One of the most outstanding Scythian kings who waged wars with Thrace and Macedon. During his reign, the borders of the Scythian state expanded considerably.

# ROMAN LEGIONARIES

### Pilum

A javelin with a long iron shank.

### Lorica segmentata armor

A convenient and reliable Roman armor made from segments — large metal plates.

The large and powerful Roman Empire was the only state in the world ever to possess the whole of the Mediterranean coast. However, it took a few centuries to create the empire within such borders. And the conquest started with its capital — Rome. No wonder gaining and guarding the borders required a lot of resources, especially human. Romans had to be at war all the time, so they had to keep a professional army. The Roman army was based on the perfectly disciplined infantry.

### Scorpio

A mechanical torsion siege engine for shooting stones or arrow-shaped missiles.

## IMPORTANT DATES

▼ **390 B.C.**

**Romans repulsed the invasion of the Gauls.**

▼ **149–146 B.C.**

**Romans destroyed the city of Carthage.**

▼ **58–51 B.C.**

**Gallic wars. Romans conquered the territory of contemporary France.**

▼ **27 B.C.**

**The Roman Empire is formed.**

▼ **378 A.D.**

**Goths defeated the Roman army in the battle at Adrianople.**

▼ **476 A.D.**

**The collapse of the Roman Empire.**

# ROMAN LEGIONARY

- Pilum
- Roman helmet
- Plated armor
- Scutum - large shield
- Balteus - belt
- Gladius - sword
- Caligae - footwear

# FAMOUS WARRIORS

**Gaius Julius Caesar**

An outstanding politician and military leader. It was Caesar who became the first commander to get the title of Emperor. While at the head of the Roman army, he conquered a lot of new territories including those of Gaul (Gallia).

# ROMAN LEGION

Enemy

Velites (light infantry)

Cavalry

Hastati (younger heavy infantry warriors)

Cavalry

Triarii (heavy infantry veterans)

Principes (experienced heavy infantry warriors)

# VIKINGS

## Bearded ax

An ax with a wide and thin blade. It was often used by Vikings because this hand weapon was easy to make.

For 200 years, in the 9th–11th centuries A.D., Europe was under attack by Scandinavian seamen — Vikings also known as Varangians or Norsemen. Those were the names for the people inhabiting Ancient Scandinavia: Norway, Denmark, and Sweden. They united in large ship parties and assaulted European cities from the sea. Most often, Vikings made a living on plundering and trading but sometimes they got hired by other countries. The strongest and the bravest of all Viking warriors were berserkers who worshipped Odin, the supreme deity of Vikings.

## "Fox head" helmet

This helmet got its name from the mask which protected the warrior's eyes and nose.

## Carolingian sword

A sword with a double-edged blade and extended fuller in the middle. Such a weapon was a privilege of only very noble and wealthy warriors.

# IMPORTANT DATES

**795 A.D.**

Norsemen first raided Ireland.

**844 A.D.**

Scandinavian warriors destroyed Lisbon, Cádiz, and Seville.

**845 A.D.**

Varangians plunged the city of Hamburg.

**845 A.D.**

Danish troops occupied Paris.

**911 A.D.**

Chief Rollo became the Duke of Normandy

**1066 A.D.**

William the Conqueror occupied England.

# NOBLE VIKING

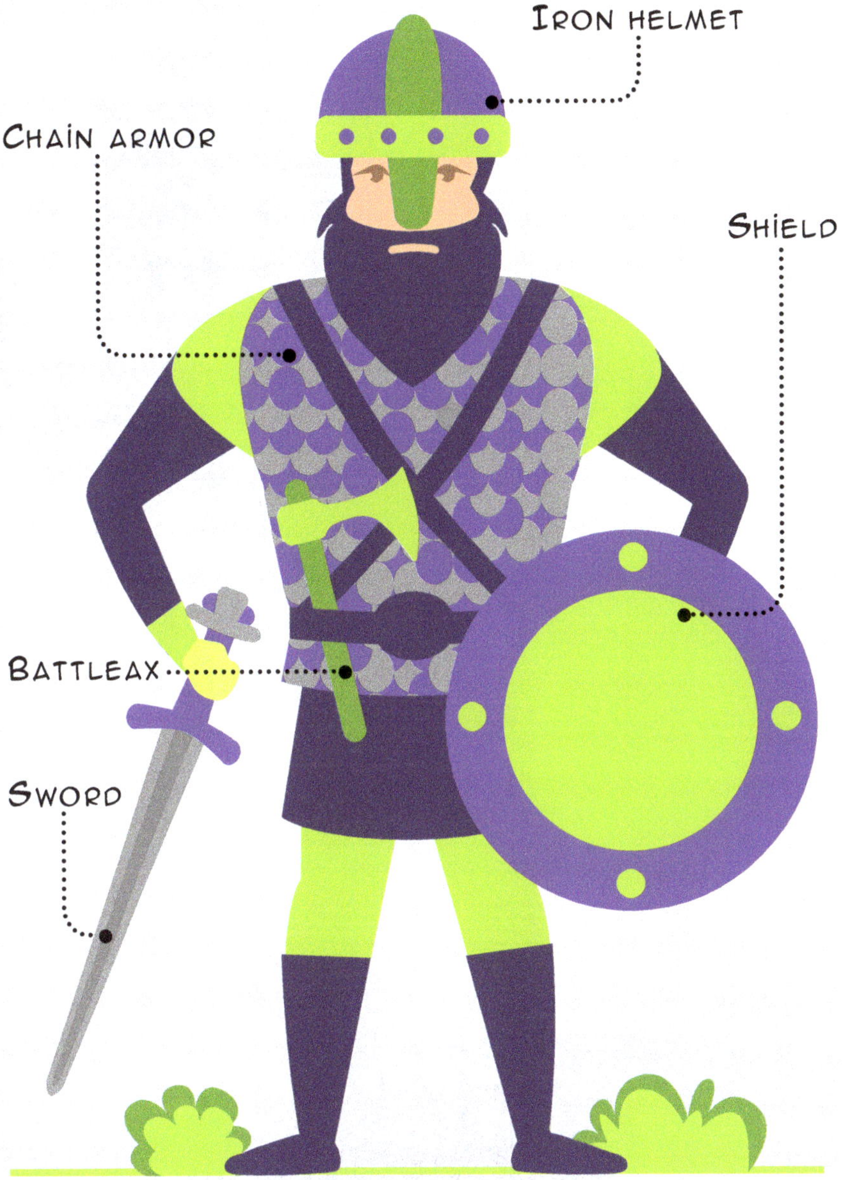

## DRAKKAR — THE VIKING WARSHIP



# FAMOUS WARRIORS

### Ragnar Lodbrok

The hero of Scandinavian sagas, war leader and konung (king) of Danish Vikings. Under his leadership, a great number of conquest raids took place. And the most famous conquest of his is the conquest of Paris in 845.

### Eimund Ringson

The Norwegian konung and the head of the mercenary brigade which was in service of the Kiev Rus Prince Yaroslav the Wise. It was he who killed Prince Sviatopolk.

# MEDIEVAL KNIGHTS

### Swords

In Medieval Europe (5th–15th centuries), the battlefield was dominated by knights – heavily armored horsemen. They were renowned for their skill, dedication, and honor. During the battle, knights lined up in rows against each other and tried to knock the rival off the horse with a spear blow. If the spear broke, they used swords or other weaponry. Medieval knights never used any range weapons like bows or crossbows as they thought it was a disgrace for them.

### Bec de corbin

The war hammer that could break through the armor.

### Heavy spear

Knocking a knight off the horse with a thin-handle spear was impossible – the spear got broken easily. This is why the spear handle was made thick and heavy.

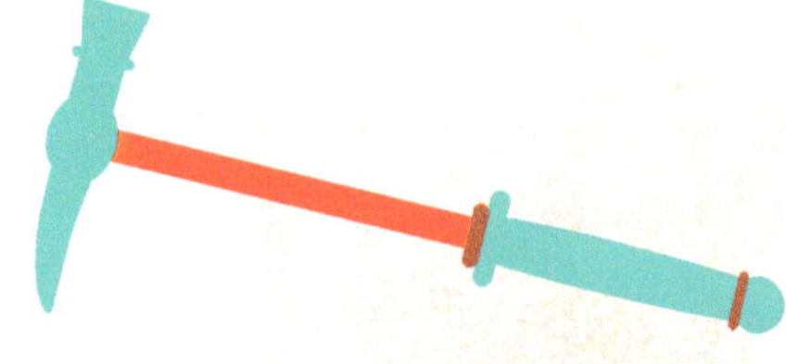

## IMPORTANT DATES

**1096**
The beginning of Middle East crusades.

**1099**
Crusaders occupied Jerusalem.

**1212**
The Spanish and the Portuguese defeated Arabs in the battle of Las Navas de Tolosa.

**1214**
The French defeated the English and Germans in the battle of Bouvines.

**1346**
The victory of the English over the French in the battle of Crécy.

**1382**
French knights defeated the Flemish in the battle of Kortrijk.

# EUROPEAN KNIGHT

# FAMOUS WARRIORS

He took part in crusades to Palestine, the main goal of which was recovering the Holy Land from Muslim to Christian rule. The crusades ended in a three-year armistice with Sultan Saladin.



# EVOLUTION OF KNIGHT HELMETS

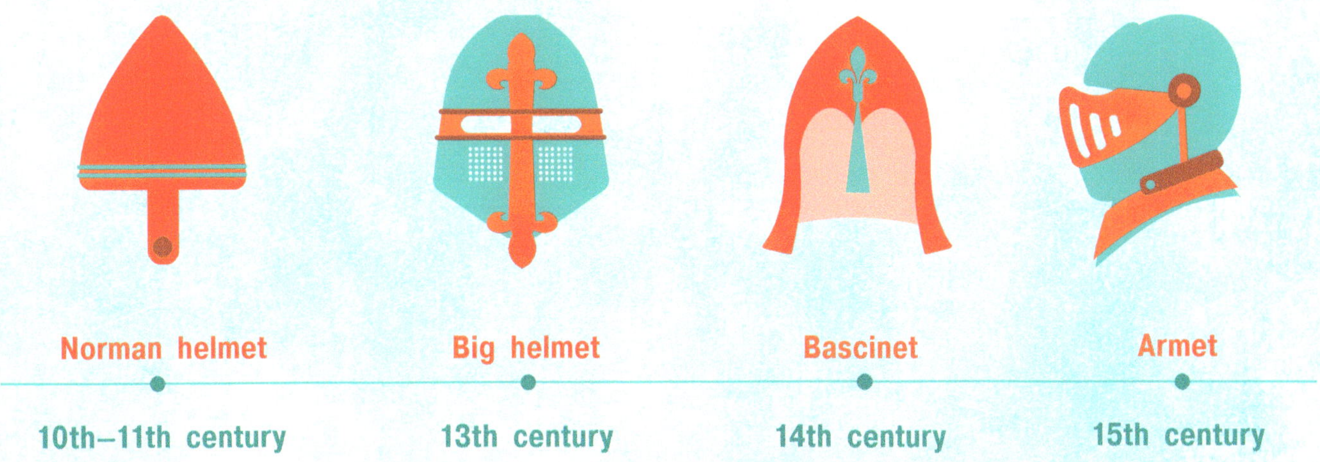

# MONGOL ARMY



## Thumb ring

Each archer was supposed to have a thumb ring with a hook, which helped draw the bowstring better.

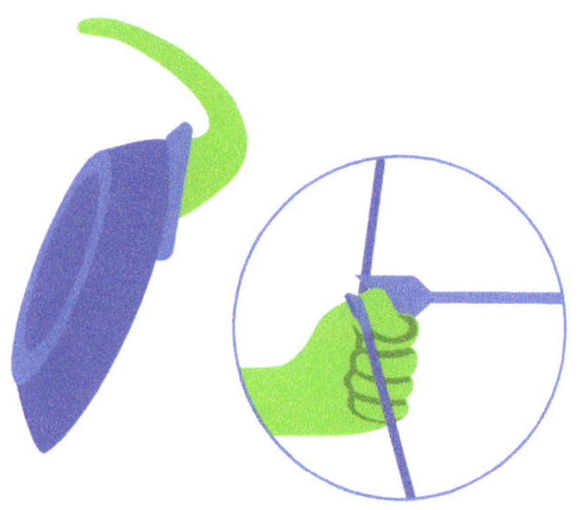

In the 13th century, Genghis-khan united Mongols and created an invincible army, the main force of which was heavy cavalry. From that time, almost all European countries suffered from the Mongol invasion. Genghis-khan's army was divided into units of 10, 100, and 1,000 soldiers. The largest unit – of 10,000 soldiers — was called the tumen. To win, Mongols often turned to a ruse by making ambushes and attacking unexpectedly. Yet, at the same time, they could easily seize a city because they had very powerful siege engines.

## Pernach

A very powerful weapon somewhat like a mace. Its blow could crush the enemy's helmet.

## Saber

A cold weapon with a curved blade used by horsemen. It could produce mighty cutting blows.

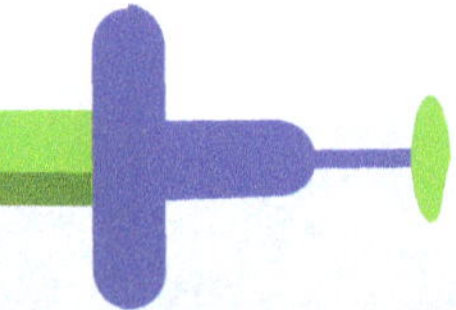

## IMPORTANT DATES

**1206**
Genghis-khan created the Mongol army.

**1211**
Mongols conquered Southern Siberia.

**1227**
Mongols crushed the Tangut kingdom in the north of China.

**1237–1241**
Mongols raided Russia.

**1279**
The Mongol army took control over all of China.

**1274 and 1281**
Sea raids to Japan.

# MONGOL HORSEMAN

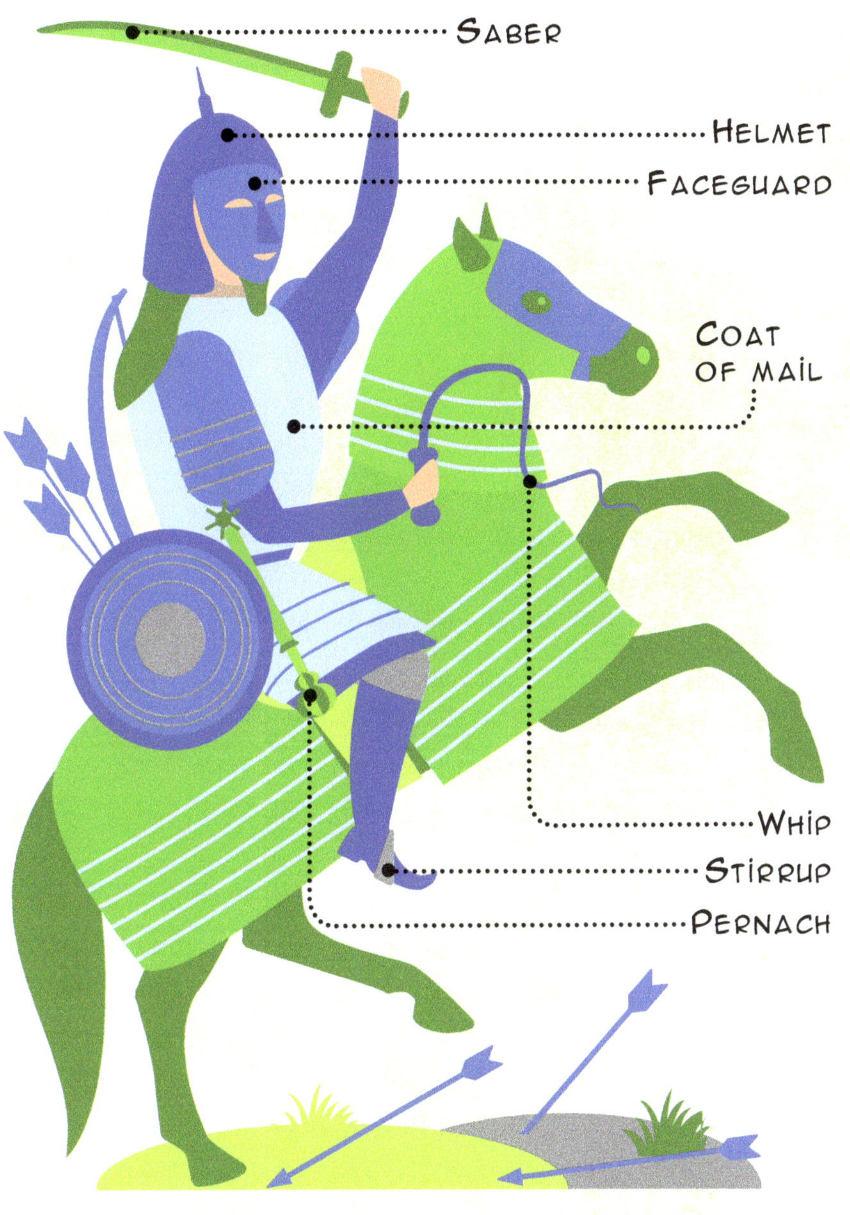


# STONE-THROWING MACHINE

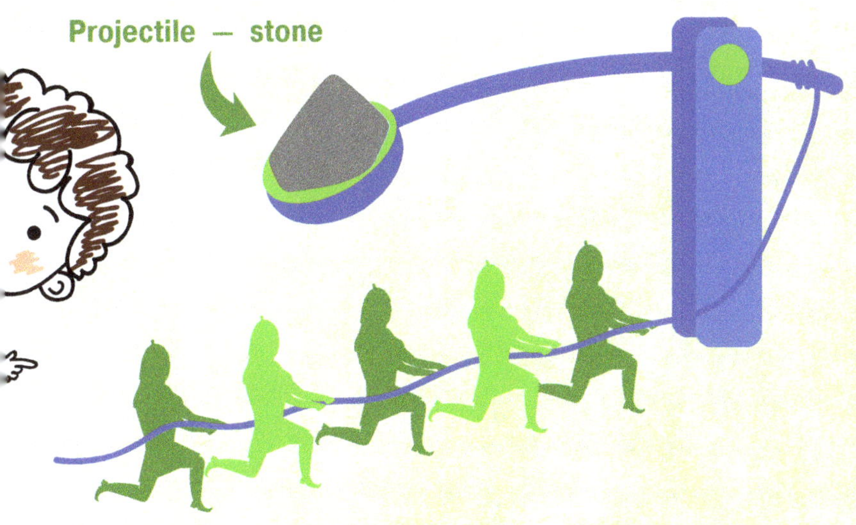


# FAMOUS WARRIORS

## Genghis-khan

The founder and the first ruler of the Mongol empire. The real name of the famous khan was Temujin. He took the name Genghis in 1206 when he got the title of the Great Khan. Having created a big and strong army, he conquered most of Eurasia.

## Batu Khan

The Mongol military leader and politician, the grandson of Genghis-khan. He led numerous raids and expanded the territory of the Mongol empire considerably. One of his greatest achievements is believed to be the destruction of Rus.

# JAPANESE SAMURAI

## Katana

A samurai's long sword. It is believed to be one of the best swords in the history of mankind.

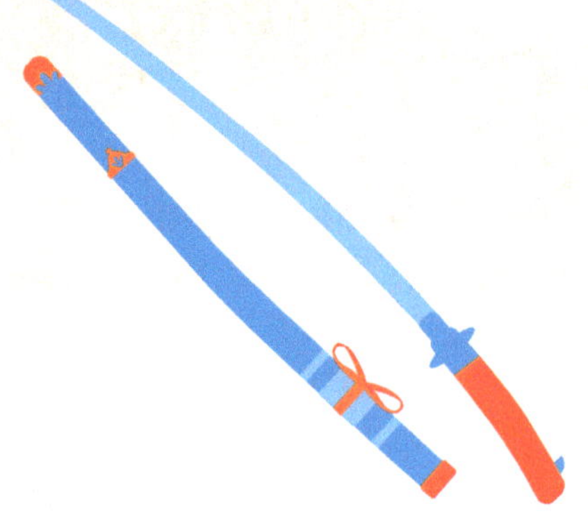

Medieval Japan was home for hereditary noble warriors — the samurai. The way of life of Japanese soldiers was to a great extent determined by the code of honor and the set of strict rules which was called "Bushido". Every samurai's morning was to be started with sword practicing. Such strict laws and rigorous discipline made warriors of Japan fearless and invincible. The only thing a samurai feared was a disgrace, for example — when displaying fear.

## Yari

A Japanese spear for parrying the enemy's attacks and attacking with thrusting or cutting blows.

## Naginata

A curved single-edged blade on a long pole. Such a weapon was extremely dangerous in the hands of an experienced warrior.

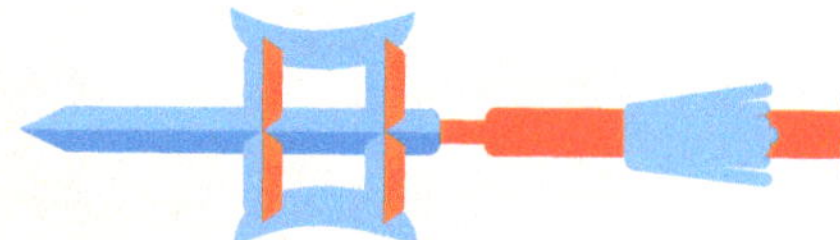

## IMPORTANT DATES

**1180–1185**
The war between Taira and Minamoto clans.

**1333–1336**
The war of two dynasties.

**1467–1603**
Sengoku period (Age of Warring States)

**1560s**
Oda Nobunaga's victory over Imagawa clan.

**1600s**
Tokugawa Ieyasu defeated the troops of Toyotomi clan.

**1615**
Tokugawa Ieyasu seized Osaka.

## JAPANESE SAMURAI

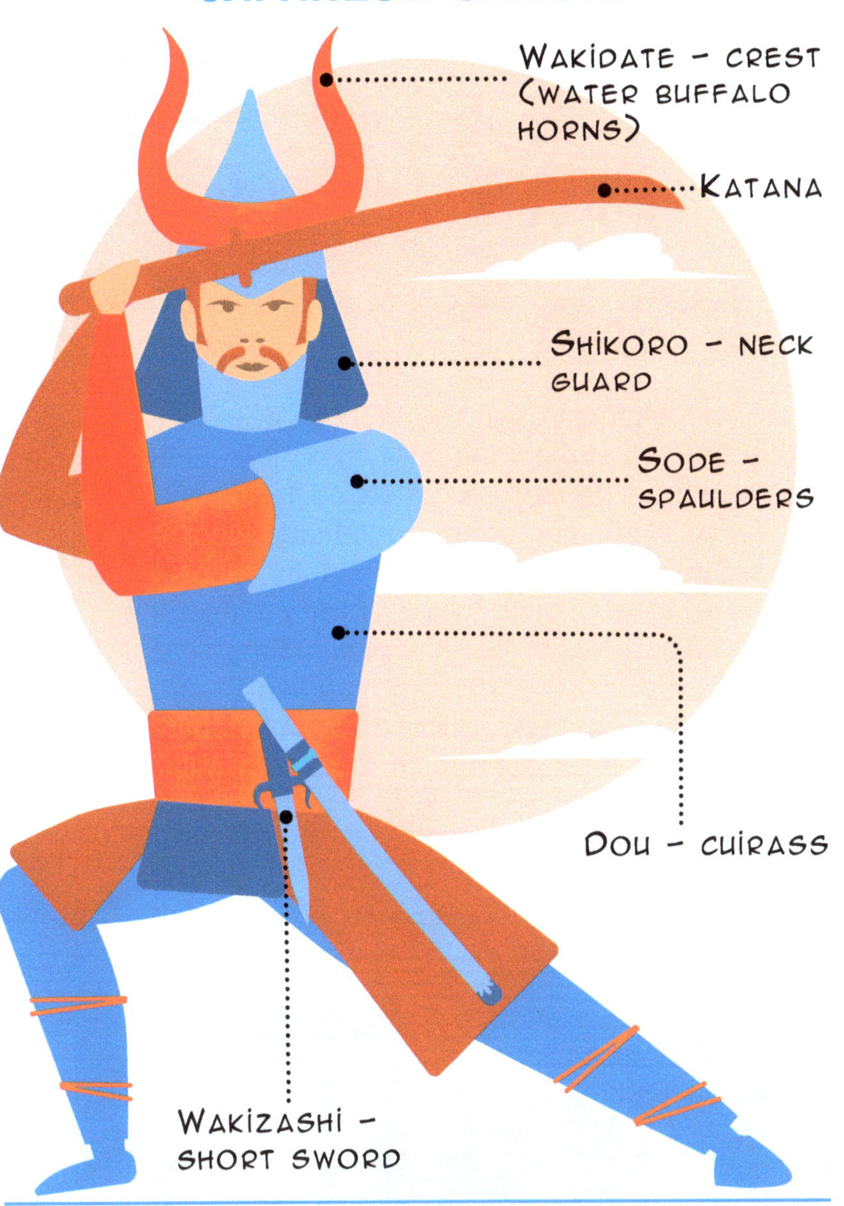


## BUSHIDO

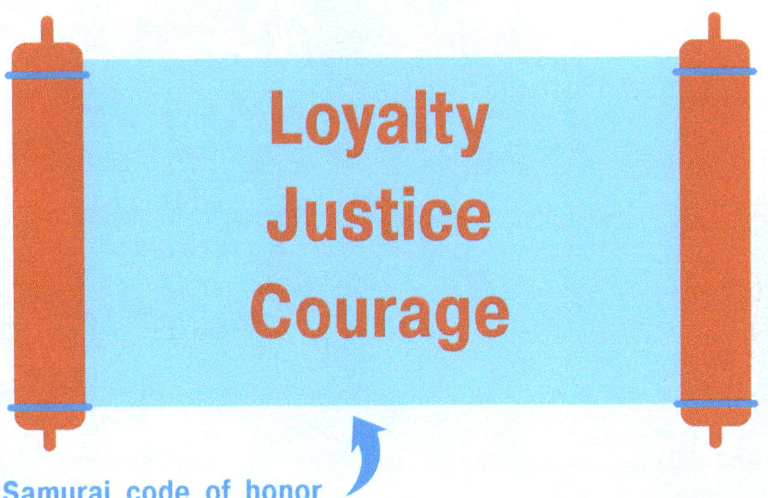


**Samurai code of honor**

## FAMOUS WARRIORS

### Oda Nobunaga

One of the most powerful rulers of Japan who fought for uniting the country. He made the army stronger and introduced new weapons. After losing the battle in the city of Kyoto, he made seppuku — the ritual suicide.

### Tokugawa Ieyasu

A famous political and state figure who managed to unite Japan. In January 1603, he became a shōgun — the real ruler of the state who de facto ruled the country instead of the emperor.

# 15TH CENTURY SWISS

## Halberd

The weapon, the head of which enabled using it both as a spear and a battle-ax.

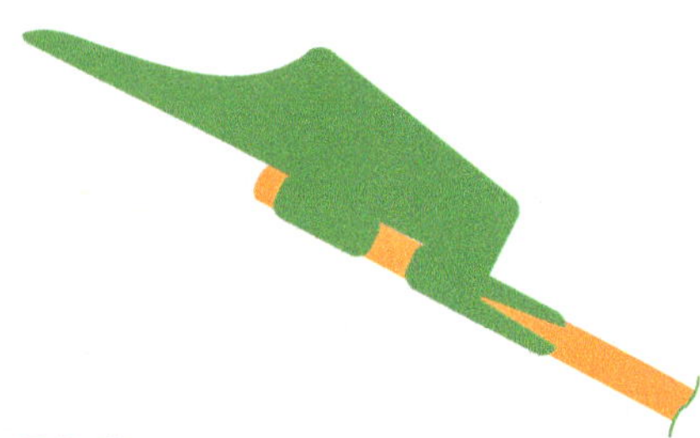

## Glaive

A kind of thrust weaponry of medieval infantry. It was used for both thrusting and cutting blows.

During the Middle Ages, the knight cavalry was so mighty that it seemed the only thing left for infantry was to defend behind the prepared fortification. But in the 14th–15th centuries, battlefields were entered by the Swiss. Those were the inhabitants of a few cantons (districts) of the Alps. They created the infantry able to resist heavy cavalry. Swiss warriors kept the order during a battle standing in large squares (pike squares). Such a way of battling influenced the development of European military science immensely.

## Crossbow

A kind of ranged weapon able to break through the armor. Yet, the crossbow had a few drawbacks: reloading it took a lot of time, and it could not shoot as far as the regular bow.

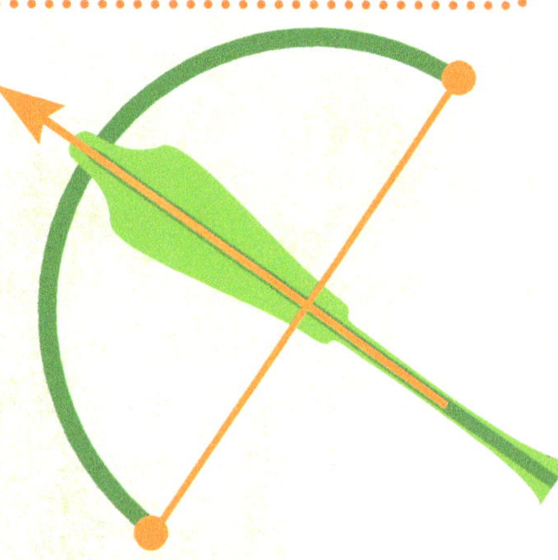

## IMPORTANT DATES

**1315**

The Swiss defeated the Austrian knights in the battle of Sempach.

**1444**

The victory of the Swiss over the French in the battle of Sankt Jakob.

**1476**

The Swiss took victory over Burgundians in the battle of Grandson.

**1494–1559**

Participation in the Italian Wars.

**1515**

The first great defeat of the Swiss in the battle of Marignano.

**1522**

The Swiss were defeated by German mercenaries in the battle of Pavia.

# SWISS INFANTRYMAN

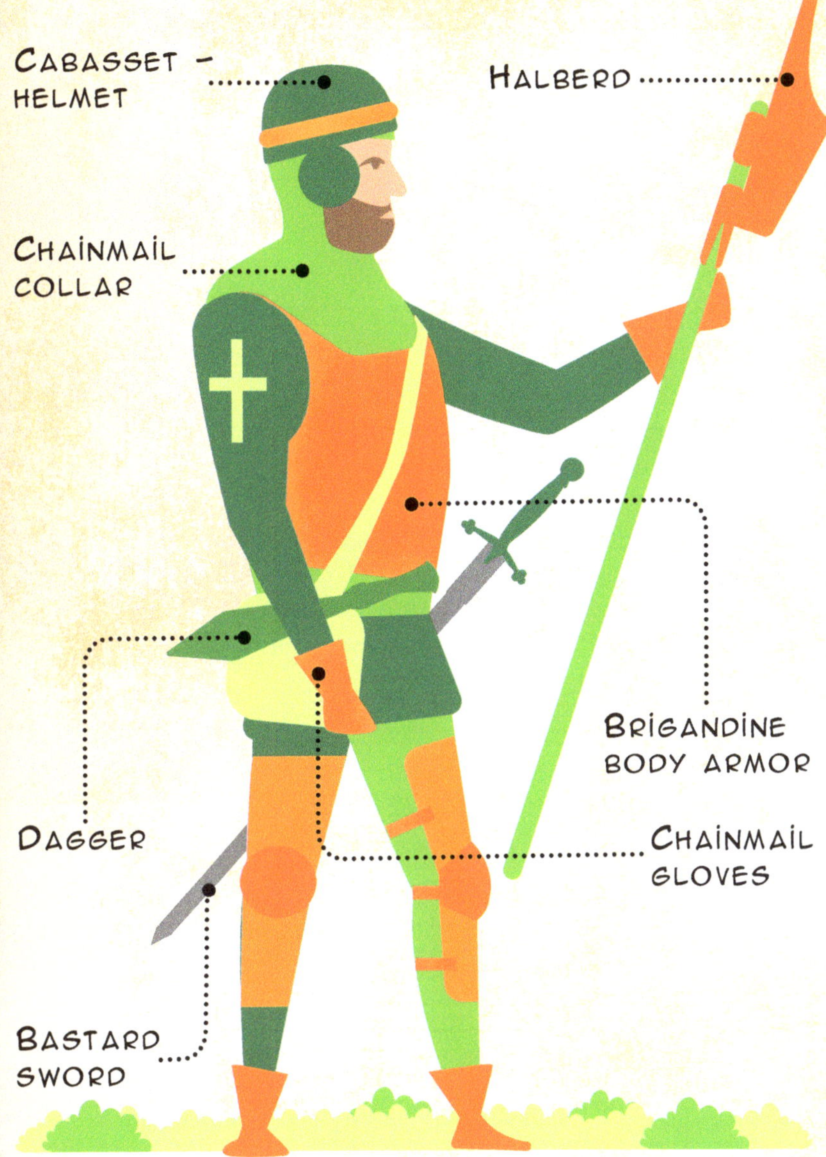



# PIKE SQUARE ORDER

# FAMOUS WARRIORS

## Werner Stauffacher

The military leader thanks to whom the Swiss army took the victory over the Austrians in the battle of Morgarten in 1315.

## Hemmann Sevogel

The hero of Switzerland who excelled in the battle of Sankt Jakob — one of the important battles between the Swiss and the French.

# UKRAINIAN COSSACKS

## Chaika

A big wooden boat which could carry from 20 to 30 warriors. On such boats, Cossacks led sea raids to the shores of the Ottoman Empire.

In the 15th–18th centuries, on the territory of modern Ukraine there was a military estate — Cossacks. It appeared at the moment when there was a need to define and defend the borders. It was this need that formed the Cossack military skill and rigor. Ukrainian Cossacks were excellent warriors, and they could fight with both thrust weapons and firearms.

## Pistol

A handgun that could shoot at a distance of up to 85 feet.

## Musket

A firearm with heavy bullets. It could get through armor from a distance of 170 feet.

## IMPORTANT DATES

**1489**
The first written record about Ukrainian Cossacks.

**1527**
Cossacks assaulted Ochakiv.

**1556**
Founding Zaporizhzhian Sich on the island of Khortytsia.

**1621**
The battle of Khotyn. Cossacks stopped the Turkish army.

**1648**
The beginning of the Cossack revolution.

**1775**
The Russian army dismissed Zaporizhzhian Sich.

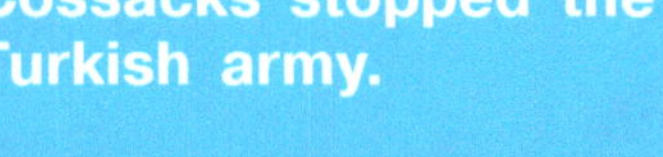

# 18TH CENTURY REGISTERED COSSACK

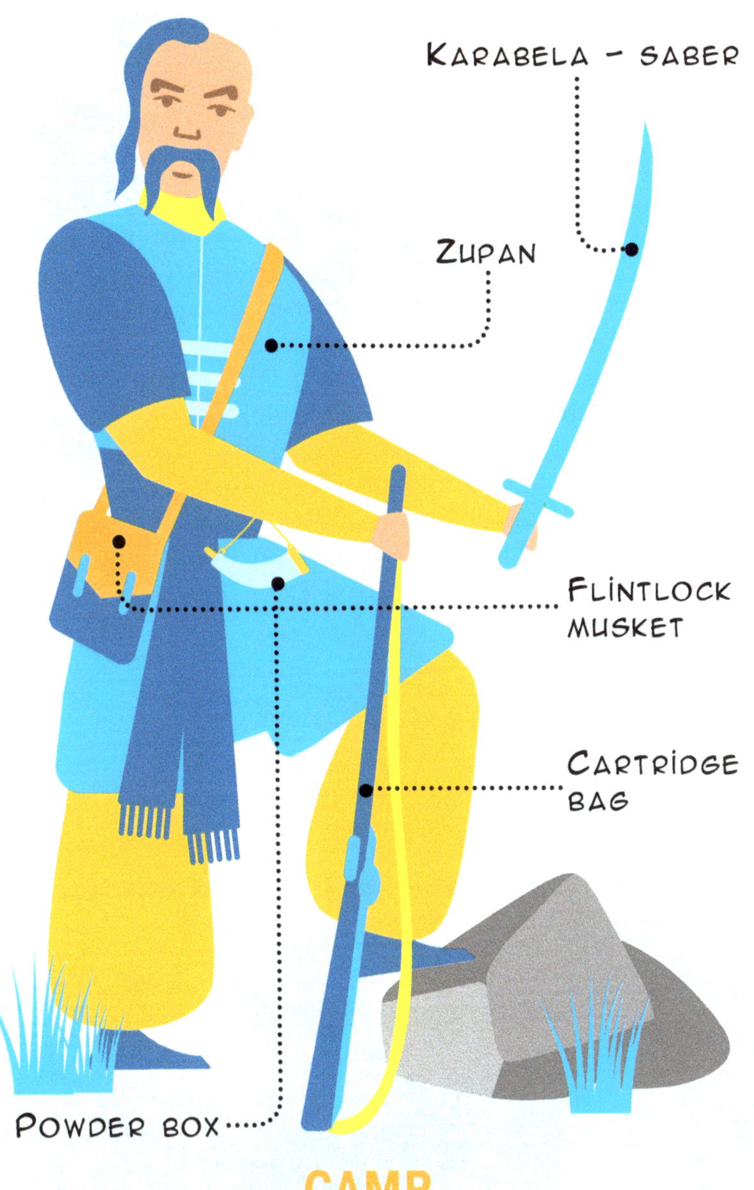


## CAMP

# FAMOUS WARRIORS

## Petro Konashevych-Sahaidachny

A glorious Zaporizhzhyan Hetman. He saw the main goal of everything he did in broadening Cossacks' rights and liberties.

## Bohdan Khmelnytsky

An outstanding political and military leader. It was he who stood at the head of the national-liberation movement of Ukrainian people. He became the founder of the Cossack state — the Hetmanate.

# SWEDISH INFANTRY

## Partizan

A kind of spear with a long, flat, and wide head.

At the beginning of the 18th century, all of Europe was seized with war, the aim of which was dividing the territory of Baltia. In this period, the Swedish army was believed to be one of the strongest in Europe. The infantry was especially famous for its order and tactics, which enabled very efficient fighting. The infantry was organized in the regiments of 1,200 soldiers. A regiment was composed of two battalions, 600 soldiers each, and each battalion – of four companies, 150 soldiers each. Swedish infantrymen used the line of battle tactic: soldiers were placed in battalion lines, between which cannons were put.

## Rapier sword

A thrust weapon with a long, narrow blade. Every Swedish military was supposed to be armed with it.

## Flintlock musket with a bayonet

Both a firearm and thrust weapon. Using it, soldiers could either shoot or fight in hand-to-hand combat.

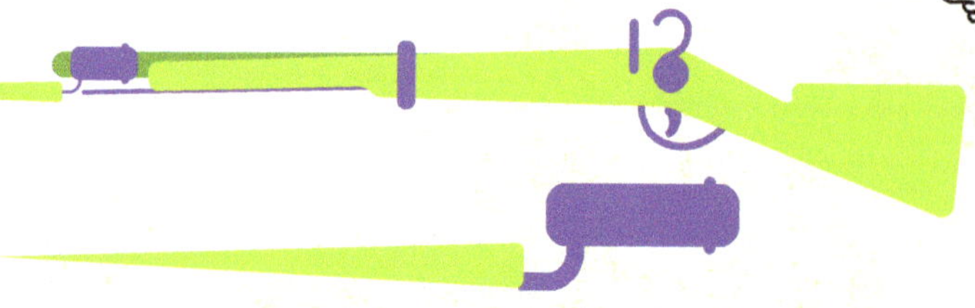

# IMPORTANT DATES

 **1700**

**The battle of Narva. The Swedish defeated the Russian army.**

 **1702**

**Charles XII of Sweden invades Poland.**

**1703**

**The battle of Pu tusk; the Swedish take victory over Saxons.**

 **1708**

**The battle of Golovchino; the victory over the Russian army.**

 **1709**

**The battle of Poltava – the greatest defeat of the Swedish.**

 **1712**

**The battle of Gadebusch; the Swedish defeated the Danish-Saxon army.**

## SWEDISH MUSKETEER

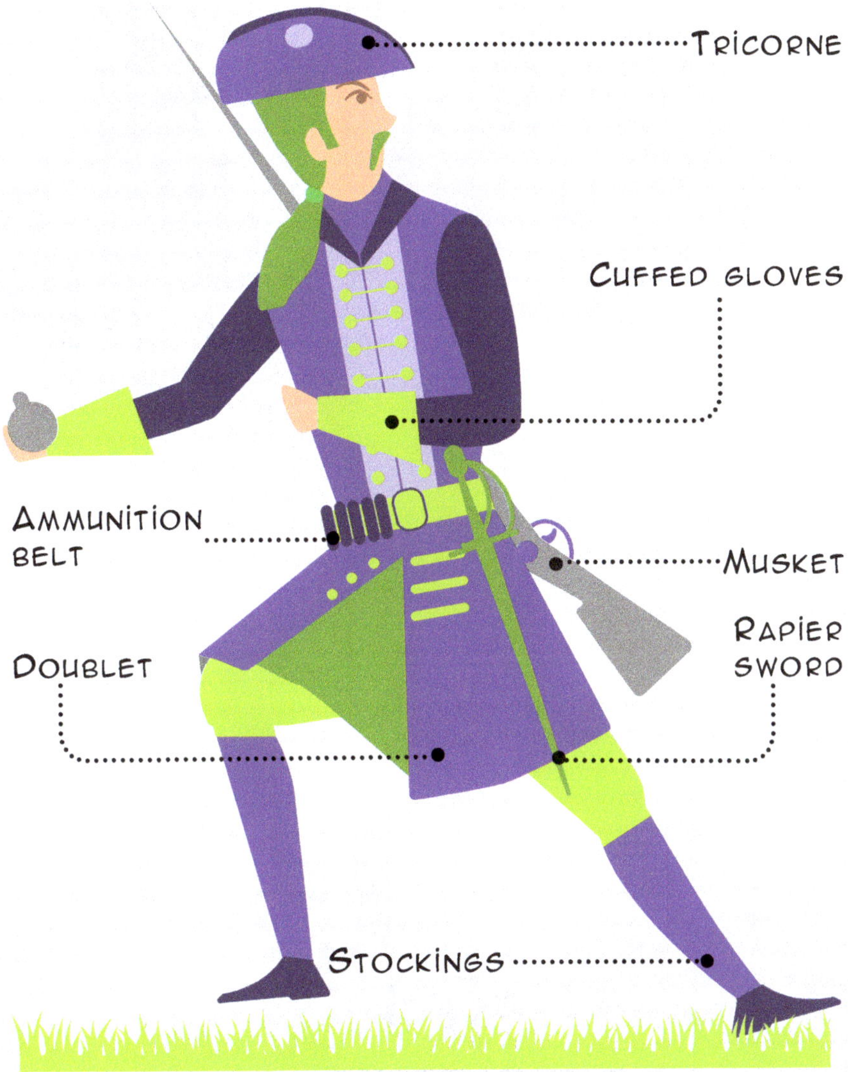
Tricorne
Cuffed gloves
Ammunition belt
Musket
Rapier sword
Doublet
Stockings

## INFANTRY BATTLE ORDER

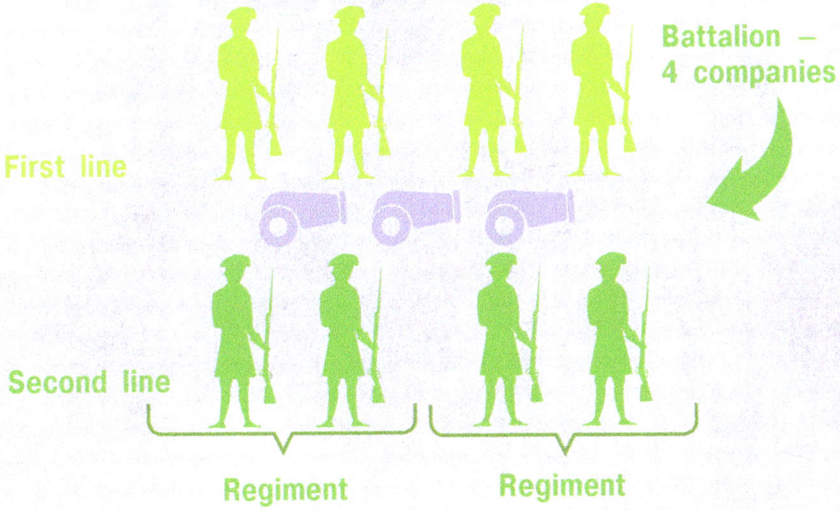
Battalion – 4 companies
First line
Second line
Regiment
Regiment

## FAMOUS WARRIORS

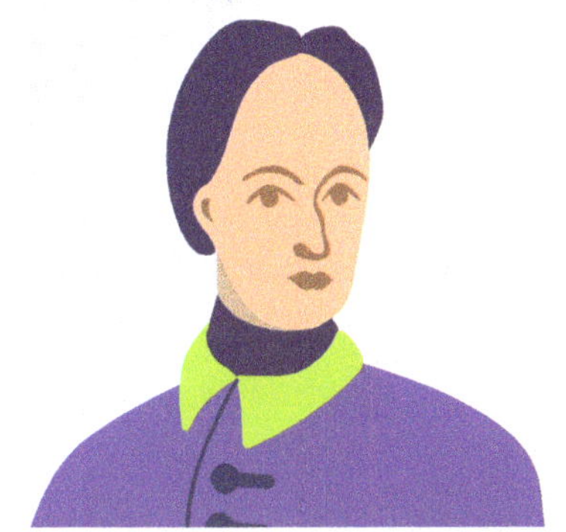

### Charles XII of Sweden

The king of Sweden and one of the best military leaders of the 18th century. Under his leadership, the Swedish army became very strong and well-organized, which resulted in a range of outstanding victories.

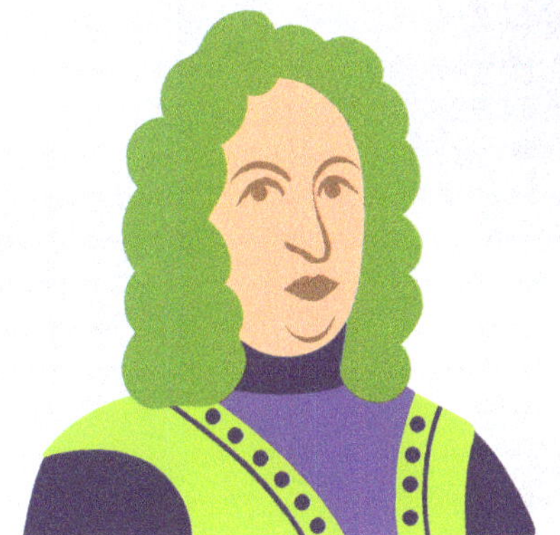

### Adam Lewenhaupt

The Swedish general and the commander of the new corps in Baltia. He had a few successful battles with the Russian army during the Great Northern War.

# NAPOLEON'S GRENADIERS

### Grenade

A hand explosive device filled with gunpowder. Before throwing it at the enemy, a soldier had to set fire to the fuse.

At the turn of the 18th–19th centuries, Europe suffered from Napoleonic wars. They were called so because all European countries fought against the Emperor of France, Napoleon Bonaparte. One of the most powerful units of his army was grenadiers. Those were infantrymen equipped with rifles, bayonets, and grenades. Only brave and skillful soldiers could become grenadiers. Very often, it happened that the attack by the infantry formed in columns determined the result of the battle.

### Broadsword

A long-bladed single-edged thrust weapon. It could make strong, cutting blows.

### Sapper ax

It was used when building field fortifications and assaulting enemy fortresses, and it could also be useful in hand-to-hand combat.

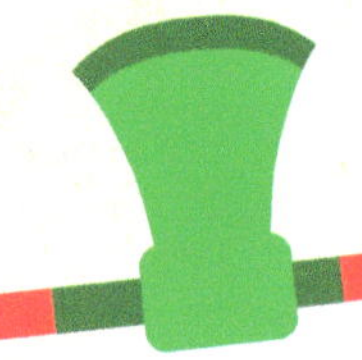

## IMPORTANT DATES

**1800**

The battle of Marengo. Napoleon defeated the Austrian army.

**1805**

The battle of Austerlitz. The defeat of the Russian-Austrian army.

**1806**

The battle of Jena. The victory over the Prussian-Austrian army.

**1809**

The battle of Wagram. Napoleon smashed the Austrians.

**1812**

The battle of Borodino — the last Napoleon's victory.

**1815**

The battle of Waterloo. Napoleon's army was defeated by the English.

# NAPOLEON'S GUARD GRENADIER

FUR HAT

HAVERSACK

MUSKET

SOLDIER SABER

EPAULETS

## NAPOLEON SAID:

Occasion governs the world.

# FAMOUS WARRIORS

**Napoleon Bonaparte**

The Emperor, one of the most outstanding military leaders in history. As a result of his numerous raids, practically all of Europe came under his rule.

**Michel Ney**

A talented commander and the Marshal of the Empire in Napoleon's army. Thanks to his determined actions, the French managed to defeat the Russian army a few times.

# FRENCH FOREIGN LEGION

## Modèle 1935

The pistol created by the Foreign Legion officer Charles Petter. The cartridge caliber was 7.65 mm and there was an 8-round magazine. The pistol was used in almost all the wars of the mid-20th century.

By the middle of the 19th century, France had gained authority over a number of colonies in Asia and Africa. The people who lived in those territories often started revolts. To fight riots, the French government created a special unit — the Foreign Legion. It had about 40,000 soldiers most of whom were citizens of different countries. Those mercenaries had their specific code of honor. They gave the oath not to France but to their unit.

## Hotchkiss M1914 machine gun

The 1914 model — the standard machine gun for the French army chambered for the 8 mm cartridges.

## Lebel Model 1886 rifle

The rifle with 8 mm cartridges and a 10-round magazine. The rifle was used by the Foreign Legion from the beginning of the 20th century.

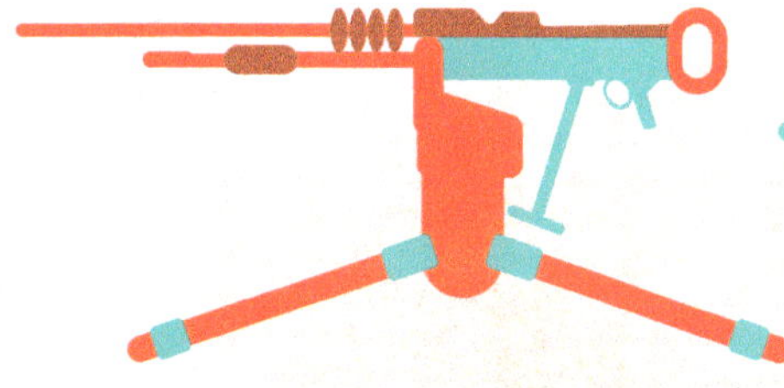

## IMPORTANT DATES

**1831–1882**
The Foreign Legion was at war in Algeria.

**1853–1856**
The legion took part in the Crimean war.

**1893–1894**
The Foreign Legion's battles in Sudan.

**1925–1927**
The Legion suppressed the revolt in Syria.

**1920–1935**
The Legion's battles in Morocco.

**1914–1940**
The Legion was holding back the revolt in Vietnam.

# SOLDIER OF THE FRENCH FOREIGN LEGION

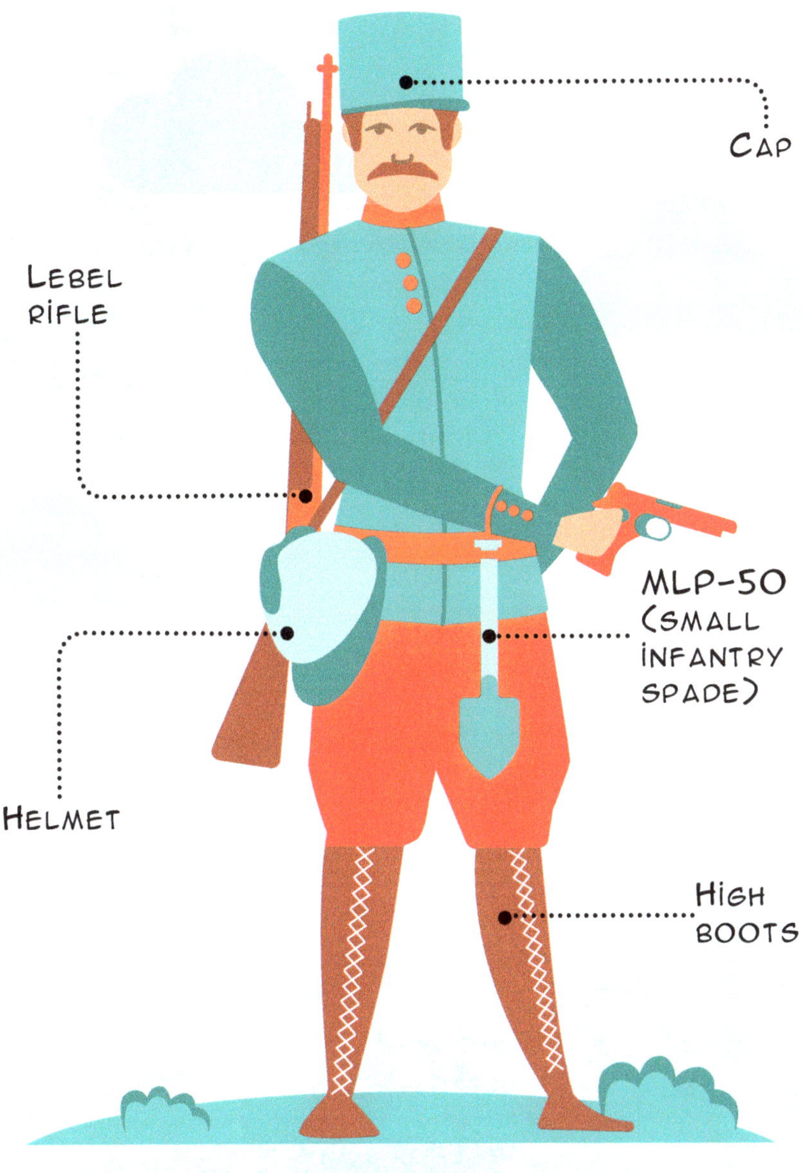


## LAFFLY 50AM

# FAMOUS WARRIORS

### Jean Danjou

The Captain of the French Foreign Legion. He became famous during the Mexican expedition of 1863. It was then that he managed to resist the attack of 2,000 Mexican patriots with only 63 soldiers at his disposal.

### Zinovy Peshkov

The general of the French army. He entered the Foreign Legion at the beginning of World War I. He became famous for his outstanding diplomatic skills and courage in battles.

# US MARINES

## Springfield M1903

The American magazine rifle. To shoot, a soldier had to move the bolt manually. The rifle caliber was 7.62 mm, and it had a 5-round magazine. At the beginning of the war, the rifle was the basic weapon of US Marines.

World War II (1939–1945) was the largest-scale war in history. The battles took place in Europe, Asia, and Africa. Very often, seashores turned into battlefields. To conduct missions like those, special forces were created. The best of those were the US Marines. They succeeded in a lot of missions: on some Pacific islands, in Northern Africa, Italy, and Normandy.

## M1 Garand

A self-loading rifle – the weapon where you just needed to pull the trigger to shoot. The caliber was 7.62 mm, the magazine contained 8 cartridges.

## M1 Carbine

A light self-loading rifle. The caliber was 7.62. The magazine contained 15 cartridges.

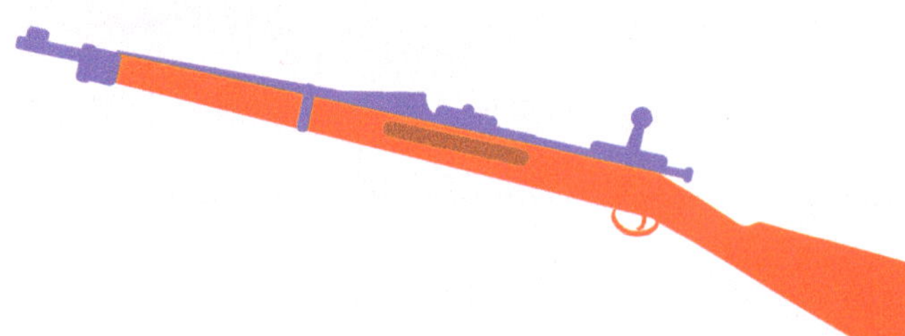

## IMPORTANT DATES

**1941**
The Marines defended the Philippines.

**1942**
The Marines took part in the Guadalcanal Campaign.

**1942**
The Marines waged an attack in Papua New Guinea.

**1943**
The US armed forces landed on the isle of Sicily.

**1943**
The Marines landed at the Tarawa Atoll.

**1945**
The Marines took part in battles on Okinawa.

# MARINE IN STANDARD UNIFORM

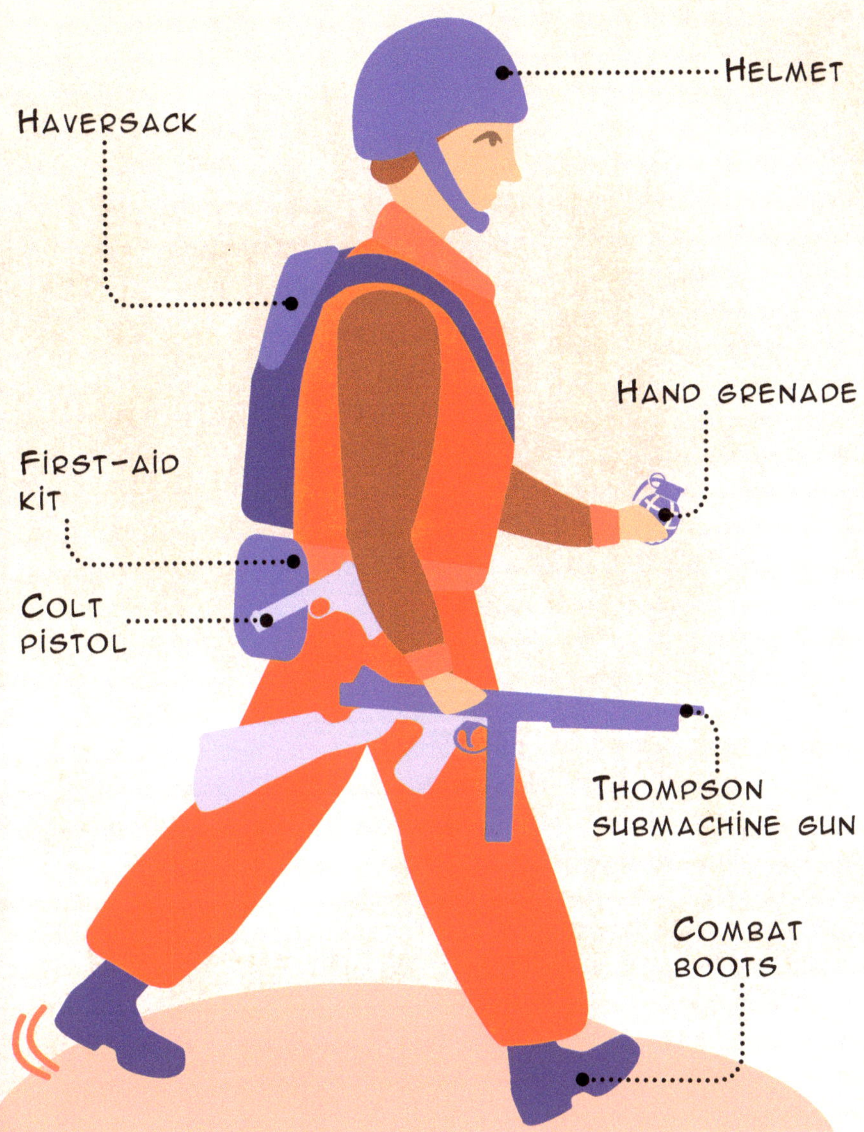



## NAVAL FERRY BARGE

**A special armored vessel for carrying Marines by sea**

# FAMOUS WARRIORS

### Holland Smith

A general in the US Marine Corps who made the Marines motorized. He provided the units with wheel and track machines. That made the Marines more mobile.

### Alexander Vandegrift

A general of the US Marine Corps. He carried out a successful land attack during the Battle of Guadalcanal. For this successful mission, he received the Medal of Honor.

# BRITISH SPECIAL FORCES

Modern armies have units for special missions. They should be able to get into the enemy's territory unnoticed, reconnoiter and organize diversions to divert the enemy's attention from the main blow. One of the most famous special forces units in the world is the British SAS. It was created in 1941 and has been engaged in practically all the wars up to present.

### Colt Canada C8A1 (former Diemaco)

A 5.56 caliber assault rifle created on the basis of the US M16.

### SA80 assault rifle

A 5.56 mm caliber weapon, created in the bullpup configuration where the trigger is placed before the magazine and the bolt.

## IMPORTANT DATES

**1941–1945**

The British SAS took part in World War II.

**1950–1960**

The Special Forces took part in the war in Malaya.

**1962–1976**

British special units took part in the war in Dhofar (Oman).

**1991**

The SAS took part in Operation Desert Storm in the Persian Gulf.

**2001–2014**

The British Special Forces took part in the mission in Afghanistan.

**2003–2011**

The SAS took part in the war in Iraq.

## L7A2 GPMG MACHINE GUN

## FAMOUS WARRIORS

One of the SAS legendary founders and military leaders. He was one of the seven British officers who received the Distinguished Service Order four times during World War II.

Lieutenant Colonel and the founder of the British SAS. He created a well-trained unit able to fight in extremely difficult conditions, for example — during the night time.

www.ingramcontent.com/pod-product-compliance
Lightning Source LLC
LaVergne TN
LVHW071005180726
843512LV00017B/1296